M000307278

This journal of **next-level encounters** belongs to:

Christ in Me: 30 Next-Level Encounters

Visit our Web site: www.grouppublishing.com

Credits:
Contributing Authors: Jenny Baker, Paul E. Gauche, Jim Kochenburger,
    and Katherine S. Zimmerman
Editor: Kelli B. Trujillo
Creative Development Editor: Amy Simpson
Chief Creative Officer: Joani Schultz
Copy Editor: Lyndsay E. Bierce
Cover & Interior Design: Liz Howe Design, with special thanks to
    Joel Armstrong, Janet Barker, and Michael Emanuele
Art Director: Jean Bruns
Design & Production Coordinator: Allen Tefft
Computer Graphic Artist: Tracy K. Donaldson
Production Manager: Dodie Tipton

Library of Congress Cataloging-in-Publication Data
Christ in me : 30 next-level encounters
    p. cm.
  ISBN 0-7644-2340-1 (alk. paper)
    1. Christian life—Meditations. I. Group Publishing.
  BV4501.3 .C486 2001
  242'.63—dc21   2001033660

Printed in Korea.
10 9 8 7 6 5 4 3 2 1   11 10 09 08 07 06 05 04 03 02

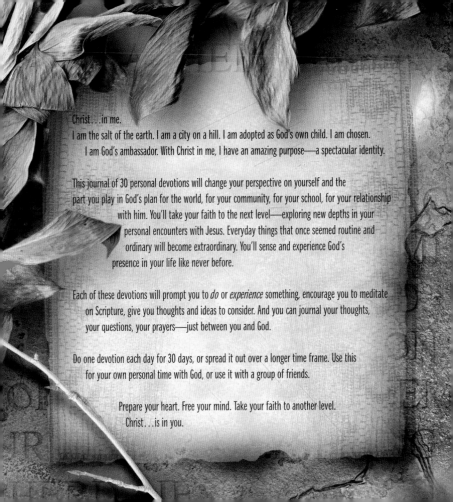

Christ. . . in me.
I am the salt of the earth. I am a city on a hill. I am adopted as God's own child. I am chosen.
I am God's ambassador. With Christ in me, I have an amazing purpose——a spectacular identity.

This journal of 30 personal devotions will change your perspective on yourself and the
part you play in God's plan for the world, for your community, for your school, for your relationship
with him. You'll take your faith to the next level——exploring new depths in your
personal encounters with Jesus. Everyday things that once seemed routine and
ordinary will become extraordinary. You'll sense and experience God's
presence in your life like never before.

Each of these devotions will prompt you to *do* or *experience* something, encourage you to meditate
on Scripture, give you thoughts and ideas to consider. And you can journal your thoughts,
your questions, your prayers——just between you and God.

Do one devotion each day for 30 days, or spread it out over a longer time frame. Use this
for your own personal time with God, or use it with a group of friends.

Prepare your heart. Free your mind. Take your faith to another level.
Christ. . . is in you.

Trophies

where the Spirit

Christ...in me.

Find a trophy, award ribbon, plaque, or certificate of achievement
that you've earned. Think back to how you felt when you were awarded the
trophy or certificate. Then recall your proudest moment or greatest achievement.

Did the "glory" of winning or achieving last or fade? Why?

What is the coolest thing you could accomplish or achieve right now?

Do you imagine the glory of that accomplishment or achievement will last?

Read 2 Corinthians 3:17-18 and Colossians 1:27.

God has given you a glory that will never fade or go away. You are being transformed into Christ's
likeness with ever-increasing glory. God dwells in you through Christ—the hope of glory.

It's nothing you have done, but something incredible that God has done for you and in you.

It's getting caught up in the constant and ongoing thrill of knowing Christ. It's about becoming
more like him. There is nothing more glorious than that. God is entrusting you to glorify Christ on earth—
to shine with his glory.

How is God's glory shining through you? (Consider for a minute or two what a privilege that is.)

How have you (or others) noticed that you are becoming more like Christ?

How are you changing and growing spiritually?

In what ways do you most long to be more like Christ? (What holds you back? Why?)

Christ's glory can shine through you as you let it,
transforming you into his likeness, drawing others to him.

Pray.

The Lord is There

Thoughts,
feelings,
musings,
dreams,
pictures,
ideas...

F R E E D O M

Christ. . .in me.

Find your passport or Social Security card. If you don't have one, look for your
school ID, driver's license, or something that shows you are a citizen of your country.

A passport enables you to travel the world. Wherever you go, it proves where you belong.

A Social Security card or ID says who you are—it's an indicator of your status.

What rights do these documents give you? What freedoms do they symbolize?
Are you proud to own them?

What responsibilities do they bring, now or later? Voting? Paying taxes? What else?

And what expectations do you have of yourself as a citizen of your country?
Does it affect the way you act, the choices you make?

Read Luke 12:27-32.

Jesus said his followers were citizens of another kingdom, the kingdom of heaven.

Without physical boundaries, this kingdom is found in every country of the world,
wherever people choose to put themselves under the rule of Christ.

It's a kingdom of different priorities—where the poor are blessed, where trust in
God replaces worry, where forgiveness is freely given and received.
It's an upside-down kingdom.

What rights do you have as a citizen of Christ's kingdom?
What responsibilities?
What expectations do you have of yourself?

And are you truly loyal to your King, Jesus? or to something else?

Reflect.

Pray.

SOLOMON
in all his splendor

Thoughts,
feelings,
musings,
dreams,
pictures,
ideas...

PASSPORT

Skin

Christ. . .in me.

Give your skin a pinch. Grab it in several places. Feel how stretchy it is, how thick it is, yet how soft it is. Look at some family pictures, and look in the mirror. How would you look without skin? How would your family look?

How grateful are you for skin?

What are some ways skin protects you (like from bumps and bruises or extreme heat)?

What if you had no skin?

Consider. . .skin is a living organ of your body. What an amazing creation!

Your skin is designed to be restorative—
if cut it heals, if burned it recovers.
It can grow back. It is designed to rebuild itself.
Your skin stretches tightly over you, very "near" to you.

Read Psalm 73:27-28.

This passage speaks of the benefit of being near to God. . .and the danger of being far away from him.

Pinch your skin again. God wants you to feel as close to him as your skin is to your body.

Christ is in you, closer than your skin, filling you, protecting you, restoring and rebuilding you all the time.

Read verse 28 again.

How close do you typically feel to God?

When do you feel closest to God?

When do you feel farthest away from God?

How close do you *want* to feel to God?

What can you do to draw closer to him—
to realize how close he is to you?

Christ is in you. Every time you touch your skin, remember that he is there with you to protect you, to guide you, to lead you, to love you—to be close to you.

Pray.

Thoughts,
feelings,
musings,
dreams,
pictures,
ideas...

IT IS GOOD

to be near God

No Answer?

Christ... in me.

Wait until after 5 p.m.—when the business day is done. Grab a phone book, and flip through the yellow pages.

Select some phone numbers of places you've been or businesses you've visited such as your school, your dentist's office, or the bank—places that are closed in the evening. Give each number a call.

What happened?

Did the phone ring and ring and ring?

Did you reach a voice mail message or an answering service?

We're closed. Nobody home. Try back tomorrow.

What if you really needed to talk to a friend, and you tried to call, but your friend wasn't home?

What if there was an emergency, and you dialed 911... and no one answered? What if they were "closed"?

Have you ever felt that way about God? Like you're trying to connect, but you just can't get through? Like you're talking into thin air?

Does God ever seem far away?

remote? silent? not there? closed?

Think of one specific time you tried to pray, but it felt like a one-sided conversation.

Now look through the phone book again—find a 24-hour grocery store, pharmacy, or even a hospital.

Would they be open if you called? What about if you called at 3 a.m.? What about 7:30? Are they ever closed?

Read 1 Peter 3:12a.

Now read it again, this time aloud.

God is *always* attentive to your prayer. He is available any hour, any minute, any second. He is never closed. He is never too busy. No matter how you may feel sometimes, he's never unavailable.

Give him a call. Talk to him right now. Tell him about your day. He's listening.

Really listening.

Pray.

Thoughts,
feelings,
musings,
Dreams,
pictures,
Ideas...

Lord are on the righteous

is ears are attentive

to their prayer

Christ...in me.

Go to a faucet, and turn on the water. Watch it run. Put your hand under the
flow, and feel it rush through your fingers. Take your hand away, and then
watch the water go down the drain, unused.

Fill a cup with water, and find a plant. You may have a plant in your home,
out in your yard, or even in a patch of grass nearby. Water your plant. See the water drip
down into the dirt. Think about how the water helps the plant grow.

Read Jeremiah 17:7-8.

A tree flourishes by a stream because it is close to its source of life—water.
You, too, can flourish in your life when you are close to *your* source of life—God!
When you place your trust in God and move closer to him, relying on him in all parts
of your life, you will grow, even in times of trouble.

Imagine yourself as a tree. God can nourish you with his love,
just like water nourishes a tree. Are you planted near God's stream of love?
Are you able to take advantage of what God has to offer?
Are your roots reaching toward the stream or away from it?
Do you trust him completely?

What might your relationship with God need to be
watered with to flourish? Do you need more prayer?
more time reading your Bible? Do you need
to make worship a bigger part of your life?

How could you learn to trust God more?

What kinds of droughts are you facing right now?
Could moving closer to God's stream of love be helpful during this drought?

Pray.

FRUIT

*Thoughts,
feelings,
musings,
dreams,
pictures,
ideas...*

Shopping

Christ . . . in me.
Go and buy something at a supermarket.
　　It doesn't have to be big—
　　maybe a candy bar or piece of fruit.
Then sit near the checkout counter, and watch other
　　people paying for their items. Who has the fullest
　　shopping cart? How do they pay—cash, check, or charge?
Now imagine what would have happened if you had walked out of the
　　store without paying. Or what if someone pushed a full cart past the
　　checkout and headed straight for the door? The cashier might shout,
　　security guards might come running, an alarm might sound . . .
Enjoy the drama of the scene in your mind—how would it end?
Read 1 Peter 1:18-20.
Paying for something means you own it—it's yours.
　　Taking without paying is theft and brings consequences.
Jesus has paid a price for you—to set you free from an empty way of life.
You belong to him—and no one can change that.
But he didn't pay with money—he paid with his own life, his own precious blood.
Because you were worth it.
How does that make you feel?
Tell Jesus about it.
Pray.

Thoughts,
feelings,
musings,
dreams,
pictures,
ideas...

CHOSEN

A Family Likeness

Christ…in me.

Find some photos of your ancestors—your mom or dad, your
    grandparents, your great-great aunt. How many generations
    can you go back?

Study the photos and look for family likeness.
    Where do you get your nose from, or your type of hair?
    Who does your family blame for your short temper?
    your height?

Some of us don't know much about our families.
    What would you like to ask your ancestors if you could?

Perhaps you are adopted—what traits of personality, taste, or
    behavior might you have "inherited" from your
    adoptive parents? What have they passed on to you?

Do you have the same hobbies or habits as others in your family?

Who has passed on their likes and dislikes to you?

Read John 1:10-13.

You are God's child, part of his family.

What family likenesses are there between you and God?

Do you share his concerns, his passions, his likes and dislikes?

How would you like your character to become more like God's?

Ask God to make you more like him.

What do you have to look forward to as a child of God?

Who else is part of the family?

Revel in the sense of belonging, of significance, of security, and of hope.

Pray.

CHILDREN BORN NOT
BUT
OF NATURAL DESCENT, NOR
BORN OF
OF HUMAN DECISION OR
GOD
A HUSBAND'S WILL,

Thoughts,
feelings,
musings,
dreams,
pictures,
ideas...

Hair

Christ…in me.

Pluck a hair from your head (or from your hairbrush). Look at the hair closely
with a magnifying glass (or a microscope if you have one). Consider the
craftsmanship that God put into that hair——the delicate structure, the color,
the curliness or straightness of it.

How important is your hair to you?

Ever had a bad hair day? a good hair day? What difference does it make?

What messages does your hair (the look of it, its style)
communicate to others about you?

Read Luke 12:6-7.

This passage contains another message about hair. Jesus
uses hair to communicate his great love for you and
his care for you. The Creator who cares about the life
and events of the lowly sparrow cares much more
about you! Every detail of your life is important.
Every circumstance. Every fear. Every worry. God cares.

What are the concerns or situations most troubling to you
right now? Share them with God.

What are the fears or worries that keep you from the
fullness of joy you can have in Christ? Tell him.

How have you questioned God's care for you?
Tell him about it now.

Close your eyes, and let God embrace you and wrap his
loving arms around you. Stay still and quiet. Ask God
to hold you. Ask him to show you ways to rest in his
hand, free from worry and fear.

Pray.

YOU ARE WORTH

more Than

HOW GOD MET ME

thoughts,
feelings,
musings,
dreams,
pictures,
ideas...

many sparrows

Clay

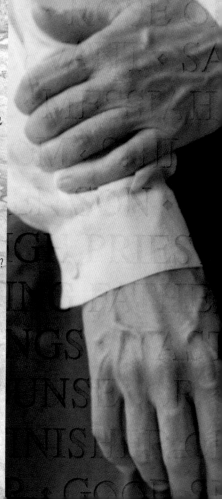

Christ...in me.

Find a handful of clay or Play-Doh. (If you don't have any, you can find it at most craft stores or at any children's toy store.) Spend some time playing—squeezing, pulling, twisting, kneading. When the clay is pliable, shape what you have into the likeness or image of one of your most treasured friends. After you've created your sculpture, set it in front of you, and read Isaiah 64:8.

Ask yourself:

"Why did I make what I did?"

"What value does this friendship have in my life?"

"What value does this sculpture have in my life?"

How would you feel if something happened to what you made?

You are God's creation, and he loves what he has made. When God looks at you, God sees an amazing work of art and says you are of infinite value and worth.

Look around your house for some finished pieces of pottery like a clay bowl, a vase, a plate, or a mug. Think about these things and how they must've brought joy and satisfaction to the artist.

Now imagine God looking at you—breathing a sigh of deep satisfaction with his finished work of art. Imagine God holding you. Think about how much love God has for you.

He is your potter.

Pray.

We are
all the
work
of your
hand

Thoughts,
feelings,
musings,
dreams,
pictures,
ideas...

Stranger

Christ...in me.

Have you ever been new to something and not quite fit in? walked into a class for the
first time and not known anyone? started a new job and felt like the odd one out?

Have you ever felt...*different*?

Go for a long walk around your neighborhood or through your downtown.
As you pass houses or buildings, consider who might live inside.

Do you know them? Do they know you? Are they different from you? similar?

If you knocked on a door, would the people inside let you in?
Or would the door stay shut?

If you walked by a playground, what would the children think
of you? Would they speak to you? Or are you just a "stranger"?

Read 1 Peter 1:17.

You are different from the people around you—God made you that way.
As his follower, your life of reverence will set you apart from the crowd.

You're an oddball. An alien. A stranger.

What makes you different?

Think about what's important to you. What do you value? How does this
affect the choices you make?

Consider your perspective on eternity. How does this color the way
you view people? material things?

What about your sense of right and wrong—your commitment to serve and
obey God? How is this different from the mind-set of your non-Christian friends?

You're called to an entirely different life—you're meant for another "world."

Do you ever feel like a stranger? So did Jesus.

Pray.

Thoughts,
feelings,
musings,
dreams,
pictures,
ideas...

YOU VALUE?

Live your lives
as strangers here in
reverent fear

Filled

Christ. . . in me.

Have you ever watched television or listened to the radio and wondered why, after watching or listening, you felt empty, confused, hurt, or even sick? Have you ever seen a movie you wish you hadn't? Have images or song lyrics ever bothered you? kept running through your mind? haunted you? Why did you watch or listen?

Turn on your television or radio, and flip through the channels or stations. Pay attention to the images and messages you see and hear.

What kinds of images do you see?

What messages do you hear?

Are they positive?

Are they negative?

Are they sad?

Are they angry?

Are they happy?

Are they confusing?

How do these images and messages make you feel?

Turn off your TV, and read Psalm 107:8-9. Notice especially verse 9.

God wants to fill your life with good things. Instead of mediocre messages, entertaining images, things that just don't satisfy. . .he knows what you need, what's truly *good* for your life.

What good things has he already filled you with? How have his unfailing love and wonderful deeds affected your life?

God wants to fill you so that when others look at you or listen to you, they will receive abundant blessings because of who Christ is, in and through you. God wants these blessings to overflow from your life into the lives of everyone you know.

You are a walking, talking, living, breathing, loving, encouraging, positive, powerful, influential reminder of God's love for everyone around you.

How can you be a blessing to someone today?

Pray.

Thoughts, feelings, musings, dreams, pictures, ideas...

for he satisfies the thirsty

THE HUNGRY

Christ. . .in me.

Read the first section of your newspaper or the headline articles from your
    Internet news service, and look for matters of right and wrong—
    people making right or wrong decisions, stuff that happened that
    was wrong or right. A crime. A scandal. A heroic act.
    Now think of your day yesterday and the right and wrong you observed.
    Did something happen that upset you? that just wasn't right?
    Did you see a good deed or observe an act of kindness?

What were some right things you heard people say or do?

What were the results of people's wicked acts or words?

What helps you determine between what is right and what is wrong?

Consider all of this.

Read Micah 6:6-8.

Some think our sense of right and wrong is proof that God exists.

You are made in God's likeness. Like God, you have a sense of right and wrong.
    He has shown you what is right.

With Christ in you, you can always know for sure what is right and what is wrong.
    You can *always* do what is right, what is just, what is merciful, with humility.

How hungry are you for righteousness?

What are some issues in your life in which you are trying to figure out
    what is right and what is wrong to do?

Who are the people and voices in your life that lead you to love what is right?
    to do what is right? How can you gain insight from them to help you?

How has Christ increased your hunger for righteousness?

When it's hard to do what you know is right, seek Christ, your righteousness,
    to guide you and to empower you to love and live righteously.

Pray.

Thoughts,
feelings,
musings,
dreams,
pictures,
ideas...

TO ACT
JUSTLY
AND TO
LOVE MERCY
AND TO
WALK
HUMBLY
WITH YOUR
GOD

Wrestling

Christ...in me.

Challenge a friend to arm-wrestle.

Use all your strength to try to force your friend's hand down onto the table.

Try again with your other arm. Which arm is stronger?

Have several more arm-wrestling matches—think of how your muscles are working.
> Does it get easier or harder to win? How do your arms feel at the end?
> How could you improve?

Now find a space to be alone, and read Romans 7:21-25.

The writer, Paul, was wrestling with doing right.

He wanted to do good, to obey God, but sin seemed stronger.

Can you identify with this? It can be hard to do what we
> know we should, even when we really want to.

Are there particular areas in which you wrestle with sin?

Who tends to win?

How can you make your obedience-muscles stronger?

Reflect for a moment.

Paul knew who could rescue him from sin—
> Jesus Christ, who defeated sin.

Ask Jesus to strengthen you, to coach you,
> to help you resist.

You may need to step back from temptation
> until you are stronger.

Take time to build up your muscles of faith.

And don't give in—keep wrestling.

Pray.

Who will rescue me fro

HOW GOD MET ME

Thoughts,
feelings,
musings,
dreams,
pictures,
ideas...

BE TO GOD

is body of death?

Being Clean

Christ...in me.

Do this meditation after some hard physical work—like playing sports,
    going for a jog, or cleaning out the garage. How does your body feel?

Now take a shower. Enjoy the sensation of the hot water running over you.
    Wash every part of your body, and get yourself clean.
    Wash your hair, your fingernails, your toes.
    Wrap yourself in a towel, and stand for a moment, enjoying your cleanliness.
    Savor the contrast between the dirty you and the clean you.

Get dressed, and read Ephesians 5:25-27.

Christ has cleansed you from every sin, every stain, every blemish, every dirty mark.

He washes you through his Word, through his Spirit.

He sees you as holy and blameless—radiant.

Can you think of things you have done that you feel
    have left a mark on you? Picture them as
    dirty stains on your body. Confess them to Christ,
    and watch them disappear as you realize that he
    has cleansed you from them.

You are clean, forgiven, beautiful—take time to let that sink in.

How do you feel?

Tomorrow you may fail, you may let Jesus down, you may become stained by sin.
    But he is always ready to cleanse, forgive, and restore you.
    Honesty and confession will keep you this clean.

Don't take that for granted.

Tell Jesus about how you feel.

Pray.

Thoughts,
feelings,
musings,
dreams,
pictures,
ideas...

rinkle...

nd blameless

Keys

Christ . . . in me.

Get out your key ring, and look at all the keys.

Which lock does each of them fit?

Now use the keys to undo all the locks you can—

maybe of doors, padlocks, a bike lock, a jewelry box, a car.

(You can lock them again when you move on to the next!)

Where do these keys enable you to go? What do they give you access to?

What would happen if you lost these keys? How much

inconvenience would it cause? Who else has copies of these keys?

What other keys would you like to own?

Think of the power that a key-holder has. Think of what a prison

warden does with his keys, or a zookeeper, or a bank manager.

Think of how much freedom one small piece of metal can

give you, or how much harm it can keep you from.

Read Revelation 1:17-18.

Jesus holds the keys to death and hell. He has the power

to keep death locked up so it cannot hold you.

He has the right to close the doors of hell

so that it cannot claim you.

Best of all, no one else has a copy of these keys!

What does this mean for you?

What difference does it make?

Rejoice in Christ's strength.

Feel secure in his care.

Pray.

Thoughts,
feelings,
musings,
dreams,
pictures,
ideas...

Then he placed
his right hand
on
me

unrise, Sunset

Christ...in me.

Plan to get up early and watch the sunrise. Then set aside time to watch
the sunset at dusk. Plan on doing this meditation at night.

How did you feel observing the sunrise and sunset? Why?

What did you think about when you observed them?

Why do you think God created them?

Read Lamentations 3:21-25.

His compassion is new every morning. Every day a new sunrise and new sunset.
A different canvas, a new portrait, no two the same.

Every sunset marks the end of an old day. Every sunrise marks the beginning of a new day.
We start the new day with a fresh new canvas, new ways to experience God's compassion, a new start,
new ways to realize God's faithfulness, new opportunities to seek God—opportunities for change.

What needs to end in your life (like sunset)?

What needs to start (like sunrise)?

What are some old sunsets that you'd like to leave behind and move on from? lingering bad memories,
experiences that made you feel worthless, hurts or pains of the past?
What old things do you need to leave behind so you can become more like Christ?

What are some new sunrises that you'd like Christ to help you move into? New behaviors,
new attitudes, new relationships, new spiritual disciplines, new ways to experience God?

Christ is in you, constantly creating new sunrises. Be sure to take time with him to see what he is
painting for you today, tomorrow, the next day. Every time you see a sunrise,
know that Christ is at work in you, creating a beautiful portrait of your day and,
as always,
a beautiful portrait of all that you can be in him.

Pray.

*Thoughts,
feelings,
musings,
dreams,
pictures,
ideas...*

never fail

I Am Covered

Christ . . . in me.

Have you ever been really cold?

Do you have a favorite blanket that you wrap up in?

When you feel lonely, tired, or even sick, isn't it nice to wrap up in a blanket in which you can feel safe and secure, as well as warm and comfortable?

Find your favorite blanket, perhaps one that you used when you were younger.

Find a place in your home where you can sit and be quiet and all alone.

Wrap the blanket around your shoulders. How does that make you feel?

Now put the blanket over your head, and let it come down around you as far as it will go.

Is it dark?

warm?

safe?

quiet?

Take the blanket off, then read Psalm 27:5.

Have you ever needed to hide?

Have you ever been in trouble?

Put the blanket back over your head. Close your eyes and breathe deeply.

Let a bit of light slip in, and read Psalm 27:5 again.

Imagine God's arms wrapping around you. Imagine God holding you, protecting you, surrounding you, covering you with love.

Know that no matter what you do or where you go, God will be with you—your shelter.

Like the warmest, safest blanket, God's love will cover you.

Pray.

Thoughts,
feelings,
musings,
dreams,
pictures,
ideas...

For in the day of trouble

Laughter

Christ…in me.

Read the daily comics in the newspaper or a comic book, or watch cartoons on TV. Enjoy what catches your eye. When you've finished, consider what you observed.

What was the funniest thing you read or saw? Why?

What typically makes you laugh?

When have you laughed the hardest? What was so funny? Did you laugh so hard your sides ached?

Read Psalm 16:11.

God has given you a path of life along with joy and eternal pleasures. He gave you laughter.

What is joy to you? What does it look like in your life?

Would you describe yourself as joyful? Why?

For what pleasures in your life are you most grateful?

What makes you happy?

Why not laugh more? What places a heaviness on you—what keeps you from laughing?

Think of the funniest thing you can recall. Laugh.

God has designed you for joy! Laughter and your sense of humor are a gift.

Jesus himself had a great sense of humor. Recall his funny word pictures like "Why do you look at the speck of sawdust in your brother's eye and pay no attention to the plank in your own eye?" (Matthew 7:3) and "It is easier for a camel to go through the eye of a needle than for a rich man to enter the kingdom of God" (Matthew 19:24b). Jesus used exaggeration to make these challenging statements easier to swallow for his listeners. Though not *hilarious* in our current culture, at the time this was pretty funny stuff! Surprising, too, from a religious teacher, since they were typically serious.

God has made you in his own image—to be joyful, with a sense of humor, to laugh! So laugh…laugh often!

Every time you feel joy in your heart, remember that it is a gift from God to you!

Pray.

YOU WILL FILL ME WIT

HOW GOD MET ME

Thoughts, feelings, musings, dreams, pictures, ideas...

Photosynthesis

Christ...in me.

Visit a garden store, nursery, or florist shop, and find a plant or a tree that is bearing fruit
(or find a houseplant or a plant outdoors that is in bloom or has berries on it).
Look closely at what is produced by the plant. Notice the colors, textures, smells,
shapes, sizes.

Does the plant look healthy? Does the plant look strong? How much sunlight or
artificial light is shining on the plant? Think about all the things that work
together to make this plant thrive: sunlight, water, soil, air.

Read Galatians 5:22-23.

Think about the spiritual "photosynthesis" in your life.

Is the light of Christ shining brightly in your life?

Are your roots planted deeply in the good soil of Christ?

Is the wind of the Spirit blowing new life into you?

What is God growing in you?

Through the power of the Holy Spirit, you can bear all
kinds of fruit. Read the list below slowly.
Think of each fruit—how is it growing in your life?

Love.

Joy.

Peace.

Patience.

Kindness.

Goodness.

Faithfulness.

Gentleness.

Self-control.

Abide in Jesus. Bear much fruit.

Pray.

Thoughts,
feelings,
musings,
dreams,
pictures,
ideas...

EAR MUCH FRUIT

A City

Christ...in me.

In the evening, go outside and sit near a streetlight. Look around you—

    do you see houses with lights on inside? Do you live in the city or in the country?

    Are there lots of lights? billboards? cars zooming by? stoplights? Or is it quiet and dark

    with just a single circle of light created by the streetlight you're sitting by?

Have you ever flown in an airplane at night and looked out the window? (If not, imagine it!)

    The earth below looks like a glowing map. Street lamps, like the one you're sitting by, mark

    out tiny dots and lines of light, with miniscule car headlights zooming up and down.

Farmland is mostly dark, with a few scattered lights here and there.

Mountains, deserts, and wilderness are invisible. Pitch black.

Cities glow. There are thousands and thousands of lights.

    Both bright and dim, both blinking and steady.

    In the darkness, they're all you see.

Read Jesus' words in Matthew 5:14-16.

You are that city on a hill—

    that landmark in the darkness that no one can miss.

    You are the glow on the horizon.

Is your light ever hidden?

    Or do you shine forth God's glory and love?

What are your city lights like?

    Are they dim? blinking?

    or brilliant?

How can you light up your school? your family?

    your community?

Pray.

Thoughts,
feelings,
musings,
dreams,
pictures,
ideas...

LET
YOUR
LIGHT SHINE
before men, that they may see
your good deeds and
PRAISE
YOUR FATHER
in heaven

The Way

Christ…in me.

Have you ever been lost?

    Have you ever been someplace that was unfamiliar to you?

    If so, then you might know what it is like to find

    your way back to more familiar surroundings.

Starting at one end of your house,

    walk to the other end using some familiar pathway.

    This is easy because you know the way.

    You are familiar with the path.

Now go back to the starting point, and put on a blindfold or close your eyes.

    Travel the same path again, but notice what you do differently:

You walk slower.

You run into things.

You're more careful.

You get disoriented.

You get lost.

Read Psalm 86:1-13. Reread verse 11.

When you know God's ways—when you are familiar with God's ways—

    you know them deep down. You know them "with your eyes closed."

    God fills you with wisdom to lead, guide, and direct you in your life.

Go back and walk the same route again with your eyes open again—

    take your Bible with you. As you walk the pathway through your house, reread verses 11 and 12.

Think about how God has led you to this point in your life.

    Consider the ways that God might be leading you in some new, unfamiliar directions soon.

    Will you trust God to show you the way?

Pray.

HOW GOD MET ME

Thoughts,
feelings,
musings,
dreams,
pictures,
ideas...

Access

Christ... in me.

Go and sit outside the office of the school principal (or college dean).

> If you're not at school, sit outside the office of your boss at work.

Who is allowed inside the office? Have you ever been inside? What was the reason?

If you wanted to talk to the principal, or boss, what would you need to do?

What would happen if you walked over, opened the door, and barged straight in?

Your access is restricted.

Read Hebrews 10:19-22.

Just for a minute, compare God with your school principal or your boss.

> God is more awesome, more powerful, more influential.

And yet your access to God has *no* restrictions. Jesus has opened up the way

> for you to go and meet with his Dad.

> There's no appointment system, no secretaries,

> no "Come back later."

Imagine yourself outside God's throne room.

> What does the door look like? There are no guards here.

Open that door and go inside—there's no need to knock.

What does the room look like?

Who else is there?

Walk toward God—he has a welcoming smile on his face.

How will you greet him?

Sit at God's feet.

What will you say to God?

What will God say to you?

Pray.

let us draw near to Go[d]

*Thoughts,
feelings,
musings,
dreams,
pictures,
Ideas...*

...ith a sincere heart in full assurance of faith

Wind

Christ...in me.

Either go outside and stand in the breeze or turn on a fan and let it blow on your face.
   Do this for several minutes, enjoying the sensation. Then go to a place where
   wind is not blowing on you at all. Take a deep breath, hold it for five seconds,
   then breathe out. Take several more breaths in the same way.

What do you like most about wind?

Have you ever been short of breath? gasped? wheezed?

What was it like to finally catch your breath? to breathe freely?

How necessary was air to you in that moment?

Read Acts 17:24-28.

In him you live and move and have your being.

In the Bible, God's Spirit is often compared to the wind. He gives us life and breath—
   and everything else. His breath of life is in us. God is so good to us.

Think of yourself as a beach ball, spiritually. Are you fully inflated in your spiritual life—
   feeling full of God's life, closely tied to him, following him closely?
   or deflated, feeling empty, disconnected, or without clear direction from him?

How are you exhaling his life out to others—
   overflowing with his love and kindness toward them?

He is not far from you. Reach out to God.
   Take a few more deep breaths. Then consider...

In what ways do you need God to breathe life into you?
   In righteousness? In love? In joy?
   In your desire to follow him and serve him?
   In knowing what it means to have Christ in you?

Let God breathe on you and bring you life in Christ today.

Pray.

For in him w

Thoughts,
feelings,
musings,
dreams,
pictures,
ideas...

...live and move and have our being.

Voice

Christ...in me.

Say each of the following phrases aloud: "Almighty God," "God loves me," "I am God's," "God lives in me,"

"I am chosen by God," and "I am in Christ, Christ is in me." Say them each again (slowly) with your eyes closed.

Listen closely to your voice, its pitch, its tone, and the power of these words.

How is your voice a gift from God?

How does God want you to use your voice?

Read Psalm 29:3-11.

God created all that is through speaking. God called everything into existence—

including you. That voice continues to direct the entire universe...and your life.

How does God speak to you? How does it affect you?

You are created in God's image. Your voice has been given power by God—

with it you can communicate God's love, encourage,

build up, create relationships...

or bring harm.

God wants your voice to be special and to be powerfully used to impact lives.

Christ in you can lead you to do amazing things through your voice.

Be still and listen for God's voice. Wait patiently. Quiet yourself.

How has God encouraged you in the past?

reassured you? communicated love? told you about your purpose?

What is God calling you to say as a voice, not an echo, to your generation?

What do you most need to hear from God right now?

(Any troubles or difficult situations you're facing?

Is there guidance you need right now?)

Be still and quiet. Listen carefully, completely, fully.

Pray.

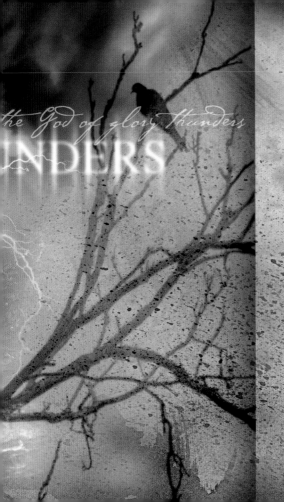

the God of glory thunders

NDERS

Thoughts,
feelings,
musings,
dreams,
pictures,
ideas...

...lose your eyes, and take a few minutes to picture soldiers in your mind—perhaps soldiers from a favorite movie, the changing of the guard at Buckingham Palace, new Army recruits marching in basic training. Could you be a soldier? Do you have the discipline?

Do these actions as you read them:

Attention! (Snap to it!)

Salute! Right face! Left face!

Attention! (Stay like this for one minute!)

At ease!

What makes soldiers so good is their obedience to officers, self-sacrifice for the cause, willingness to lay down their lives for others, self-discipline, and knowledge of the art of war.

How are you most like a soldier? least like a soldier?

Read 2 Timothy 2:1-15. Reread verses 3-4.

Spiritual life demands the same things that make a soldier good: obedience to God, self-sacrifice for the goals of God and the kingdom of God, a willingness to lay down one's life (your own needs, your own plans) for the cause of the gospel, self-discipline and the practice of spiritual disciplines (like prayer and Bible reading). A soldier of Christ Jesus is trained and ready to oppose evil.

How would you rate yourself as a "soldier" for Christ?

What are you enduring for Christ?

Who are the people who bring out the "soldier" in you and inspire you as a Christian? Why?

Imagine the soldier in Christ you would most like to be…

What one thing can you begin doing to become that soldier?

What one attitude can you change to become that soldier?

Christ is in you. Every discipline, every right action or attitude, and every bit of energy you need to endure the harshest of life circumstances can be found in Christ. Every desire to do what is right, everything you need to be self-disciplined and totally sold out to Christ is in you. Ask God to make you a soldier through Christ's power.

Pray.

Thoughts, feelings, musings, dreams, pictures, ideas...

Jesus Christ,
raised from the dead,

nded from David.

Tools

Christ . . . in me.

Visit a store where you'll be able to find tools (or look
at your mom or dad's toolbox in the garage). Gather
some common tools like a wrench, a screwdriver,
and a tape measure. How is each one used?

Now find some tools that are less common, like an
oil filter wrench, a wire stripper, a Sheetrock saw,
or perhaps a tool you don't even recognize.
Look at the tools, and notice how each one is
made for a particular purpose. You cannot use an
oil filter wrench to tighten a bolt. You cannot use
a screwdriver to measure the length of a board.
You cannot use a Sheetrock saw to strip a wire.

Read 1 Corinthians 12:4-11.

God has given every Christian certain gifts to strengthen
the whole church. What were you created to do?

Are you smart?

Are you trustworthy?

Are you faithful?

Do your friends find your friendship healing?

Do you serve others with joy?

Does your kindness touch lives?

God has given you gifts to use to strengthen those around you.

Put away or return your tools. As you do, thank God that each
one of us has different gifts which work together to
strengthen the Body of Christ. Ask for the courage to live
out your purpose—to actively use your gifts to change lives.

Pray.

Now to each one th

*Thoughts,
feelings,
musings,
dreams,
pictures,
ideas...*

*...manifestation of
...e Spirit is given for*

common good.

Dirt

Christ . . . in me.

Go to a place where dirt can be found. Pick up a handful of it. Feel its texture.
  Rub it between two fingers. Let it slowly sift through your fingers.

It's filled with the nutrients necessary to nurture life and to bring growth.

What is like dirt in your life? What is bringing you life?
  causing you to grow?

Who are the people who help you to grow?

What are you doing to grow?

Think of all that God is doing to cause you to grow—
  for the many ways God is bringing you life . . . (Take your time.)

Read Matthew 13:1-9, 18-23.

What kind of soil are you planted in?

What is good that is growing in your life?

What is growing in you spiritually?

Are there any weeds in your life that are trying to choke out
  your love for God? your drive for righteousness?

How will you uproot them?

Pick up another handful of dirt. Hold it tight in your hand.

How would you like to grow to become more like Christ?

Will you be a young sapling? or a mighty oak?

Christ is in you, like a seed. Everything you need for an abundant,
  fruitful, joyful life is in him, in you. Allow him to mold you and
  shape you to be more like him—to uproot the bad, to plant
  and fertilize the good. Allow Christ to "grow" in you.

Pray.

Thoughts,
feelings,
musings,
dreams,
pictures,
ideas.

yielding

a hundred,

sixty or

...E PRODUCES A CROP.

thirty times

what

was

sown

Many Parts

Christ… in me.

Stand in front of a full-length mirror. Look at yourself, and examine the many parts
of your body, head to toe. Put your hand up to your heart and feel it beating.
Put your hand out in front of you. Examine your fingers, and imagine your blood
running through them. Walk in place for a moment, and watch how all the parts of your body
work together to make that movement possible. Stand quietly.
What are you thinking? feeling?

Your body works as a unit——
to make movement,
think thoughts, and create feelings.

Read 1 Corinthians 12:14-27.

Think about the worldwide community of believers in Christ——the body…
the many parts. How many do you think there are? Where do they live?

What is their daily life like? How are they like you?
How are they different from you?

We all work together with other Christians to build Christ's kingdom.
We need everyone's gifts and talents to spread God's Word to all nations.

Go back to looking at yourself in the mirror.
What does your hand do to further God's work here on earth?

Your feet?

Your head?

Your heart?

What could you do to work with the worldwide community of believers
and spread God's Word?

What could you do at your school? with your church? at home? in your community?

Pray.

Thoughts,
feelings,
musings,
dreams,
pictures,
ideas...

BODY of CHRIST

Painting

Christ . . . in me.

Choose something to paint——it could be a scene, a person, an object, or an abstract picture.
  Use just black and white for your painting——how many shades of gray do you need
    to make? Take some time to produce a picture that you are pleased with. (You could
    use colored pencils or crayons instead of paints if that's easier.)

Now take a fresh piece of paper and a whole range of colors.
  Paint that same picture again, but this time use as many colors as you can.

Enjoy the contrast of different shades, the richness of the different hues,
  the freedom of choosing the exact color you need.

Sit back and compare your two paintings.

Read John 10:7-10.

Many people see God as restricting, expecting his people to live a
  gray life like your first painting, full of rules, with all color removed.
    Is that view right?

Jesus came to give us a full, vibrant, multicolored life——life in all its fullness.

Think of the blessings that knowing Jesus brings——imagine each one
  as a color. What shade will you choose for forgiveness?
    love? acceptance? purpose?

Look at your second, colorful painting——see those blessings interwoven
  in the picture, contributing to its beauty.

Thank God for his rich gift of a creative, abundant, vibrant life.
  Ask him to help you discover more of it.

Paint another picture to express your praise.

Pray.

Thoughts, feelings, musings, dreams, pictures, ideas.

THEY MAY HAVE LIFE,

and have it to the full.

Stirred Up

Christ...in me.

God is at work in you through the power of the Holy Spirit.

Even when you don't feel like much is going on, God's Spirit is
moving, bubbling, welling up from the very depths of your life.

Take two pans, and fill each of them with water. Set each of them on the stove, and carefully turn one of the burners
on high. As the heat begins to warm the water and the one pan and finally comes to a boil, watch what happens.
What do you see?

Bubbles...steam...movement...rippling water.

Now look at the other pan of water—the one without any heat under it. What do you see? What don't you see?

Read John 5:2-9.

After thirty-eight years of waiting—waiting to experience the miraculous...

to submerge himself in the stirred-up pool—a man's life was dramatically changed.

He experienced the love of Christ bubbling up in his life!

God wants our lives to be like the water that is stirred up.

He wants us to provide hope for the lost, rest for the weary.

He wants to fill us with the miraculous.

Look again at both of the pans of water. The more the pan is exposed

to the heat, the more dynamic it becomes:

With Christ you can

bubble...with joy,

shake...with excitement,

move...with power,

live...with purpose!

What are the ways that this is happening in your life today?

How can he overflow in your life?

Pray.